ALEX FORREST

52 First Dates: Part 3 of 12

A Memoir & Dating Handbook

Contents

Note on Book

*Alex Forrest is a writer and lawyer, whose first book, "**Too Late, Mate?**" covers the 18-month period in which he first learned a technique for approaching women in the daytime called "daygame." This 12-part ebook series documents the next phase of his adventures in which he goes on 52 first dates in a year, once more putting the teachings of the pick-up and seduction community into practice. Alongside the entertaining stories, it also features special sections describing in detail the methods and skills used.*

Dates 5 & 6: Young & Gauche

I have put these dates together because they were both young women, probably in their early twenties, and both attended University, or at least recently graduated in the case of Date 6. They were also young in a different way, in so far as they were not quite conscious of the power of their own sexuality and seemed somewhat "gauche" and inexperienced. One was a lawyer, one an academic. They were both reserved, shy, and uncomfortable with dating. And yet some sort of attraction had been triggered in them by the directness of my initial approaches during the daytime, in two separate shopping centers in Warsaw.

Date 5 was a 22-year-old blonde girl and had been so struck that she agreed to an instant date without much persuasion. She was drifting dreamily along on a Sunday afternoon staring into shop windows, looking lovely in a very revealing black and white striped dress with shoulder straps, and she was somewhat unaware of her own attractiveness. She was innocent (almost), as if she had only just recently taken possession of her sexuality.

The instant date at an adjacent Costa Coffee was very clunky. It was clear that this had never happened to her before, and she had probably gotten more than she had bargained for that day. I felt that it was very likely that she had spent most of her

1

adulthood to this point with her head in her books and doing little in the way of dating and certainly even less in the way of flirtation and seduction. The black and white striped dress with the low straps felt like a sudden, bold decision to experiment. Almost as if she was only just coming into her womanhood at a late stage, and something in her, some primal, subconscious force or urging, had led to the decision to dress up on a Sunday and swan around a shopping center.

Many younger girls really pay little attention to what drives them. They strike me as butterflies who simply cannot help fluttering about in an attempt to draw attention to themselves (quite rightly so) but have absolutely zero idea of the powerful biology that they are in fact in thrall to. Especially so in the case of academic or intelligent girls whose head cannot square the circle with their heart, of course. Although heart is the wrong word. It is their primal instinct, their biology that they are struggling with and alarmed to find themselves in the grip of. In the case of this butterfly, I almost expected her to be carrying a school book and wearing spectacles. It was not that she was young, so much as she was not sexually mature.

The instant date was, as I said, pretty clunky. She was clearly in the category of "Hot Academic" as she spoke five different languages. (How is that even possible at such a young age?) As we chatted, the impression was reinforced that she did not get out much, although it was clear to me that she was definitely now reviewing her life decision to be a bookish-student and was starting to try to spread her wings.

Still, the date was hard work, and, perhaps to my discredit, I bailed after about 40 minutes because of this. There is also a part of me that was not hugely attracted. I do not mean to say I would not sleep with her. I would have done. But for the amount of investment it would have probably taken to get to that point, it did not seem worth it. This is why more mature girls can often be rather more interesting to men, at least to me, especially if they stay in shape.

Men can be lazy beasts, and while they might lick their lips at the prospect of the hunt upon seeing an attractive young antelope pop out of the long grass, the amount of effort required to chase it down – and the amount of dancing about it does– suddenly turns the whole enterprise into an exhausting project in their minds. So instead, they roll onto their back and decide on a snooze instead!

Date 6 was indeed very similar to Date 5, although she had recently graduated and was in a job. She was a Polish girl from a city called, Bialystock. I wish I could show you her Facebook profile. She looks like a doll. Strong red lipstick and curly fair hair, lots of it, like a mannequin in a shop window. It's as though her mother just bought her the "Girl's Book of Beauty" for Christmas, and she is trying out different styles. The day I met her, she was on Page One: "How to look stunning on a date." Although judging by her later appearance on the date itself, I think she had drifted onto Page Eighteen, "How to dress for a dinner party with the Royal Family." A part of me imagined her still a girlish teenager, rummaging through her mother's wardrobe, trying on her mother's shoes and clothes far too large for her.

I first approached her at the bottom of an escalator in a shopping centre, and she really was wowed. I think it was the way that I just sort of "pounced" by jumping in front of her without a moment's thought. My attention had been immediately caught by her young beauty and her makeup looks.

(I am as much a victim of my biology as she is of hers.) I went straight into my flow and had an excellent vibe. It reminded me of something I had heard the famous Yad (he of the early Daygame.com days) say: "If the vibe is right, you can literally get away with anything."[1] And I think this was the proof of that statement in action. I was a much older guy, and here she was, a young women of barely more than 22 or 23 years (a big age gap).

She was very circumspect in the texting in between the approach and the date. When I asked her out, she texted, "I'm too young for you, but ok." In fact, after the very first text I sent her, she actually sent the same text twice, the second text simply being to correct a spelling error in the first and to apologize for it! She was afraid of meeting me, partly because of her English.

* * *

The date itself bore out her inexperience. She dressed up in a very posh dress and high heels in spite of the fact we met for coffee on a Sunday morning in Cafe Nero in a shopping center. It cannot have been much later than 11:30 am, perhaps the earliest date I have ever had.[2]

"Logistics," as PUAs say, became a problem with this girl as she lived in another city and only came to Warsaw once a week,

---

[1] I have done a podcast with Yad on the origins of daygame, which you can find on my YouTube Channel.

[2] You can actually see a still of her if you watch the YouTube video on my channel.

usually on the weekends. So this was why we ended up with an unusual date on a Sunday morning.

It was immediately quite awkward, and I was struck by the amount of makeup she had on. I felt like telling her, "You're quite attractive already, you know, and anyway, I'm one of those guys whose more into a girl's figure than a pretty face." But this would have been a rather bold statement to a girl right at the beginning the date!

The awkwardness of the situation was not helped by the fact that we sat in chairs across from each other at a cafe in a busy shopping centre. The chairs were deep and you sunk into them. It would have taken a cherry picker to get us out of our seats they were so deep! And because of the very busy and public location, there was very little opportunity to touch or to have any intimacy of any sort.

She sat the whole time with both her bag and her coat on her lap, as if she might finish the date at any minute. So I manfully carried the conversation as best I could. It ranged over an array of topics that did not yield much, and I started to wonder whether the problem might be her English. I do talk quickly, and maybe she was so nervous because she was struggling to follow me but too polite to say anything.

Eventually I stopped talking. It just felt like one of those old-fashioned dates I had been on where you just talk for the sake of talk because you are uncomfortable about silence. But silence was hard work too. Poor girl. I almost felt sorry for her, sitting there struggling to deal with a guy twice her age, waffling along in a foreign language, a victim of her biology which meant she had pretty much no choice but to want to meet me and come out because of the primal attraction I had generated in the street.

Like Date 5, she was an intelligent, educated girl, and she might have been totally at sea, a whirl of conflicting emotions, her head and heart in fierce competition. She reminded me of myself, in fact, as a younger man, incapable of exerting any sort of control of structure onto a wacky, crazy situation like a date, in which of course so few of us are given any real training.

However, I was no longer that young man, and I had some training. I managed to find my bearings and ask myself mid-date, *What now? What's my next step?*

It was clear to me that I needed to take action, some sort of action, and I had reached that moment before with Date 4.[3] It was now becoming obvious to me that it is the taking of action that women are attracted to, and it hardly matters what action you take. I had to change things up, spin things around. There is perhaps nothing *less attractive* than a ditherer on a date. Even an asshole, in spite of a woman's protests, is probably better than a ditherer. At least she knows where she stands.

Anyway, while ranging across a wide range of topics, desperately looking for some common interest, I stumbled on one in skiing. But because conversation was so clunky and had almost run dry, either because she did not understand my English or just because she was painfully shy, I yanked myself out of the depths of my comfy sofa chair and grabbed a chair from another table and came and sat next to her.

I produced my mobile phone.

Remind me never to select sofa chairs like this again, I said to myself, as I scrolled through photos. *They are death to a date. Not only are they deeper than the Saint Antonio trench, but they*

---

[3] In the case of Date 4 you may recall that I just got up from my side of the table and walked around to hers, moving her handbag in the process so I could get closer to her.

have these stupid curved arms that make it impossible for you to get anywhere near the girl.

The phone idea turned out to be a good one. I recalled some advice from a PUA who had said that you need to have a good collection of photos on your phone for this very eventuality or where a girl speaks very little English. I showed her photos of my recent ski trip. At last we had something to gush about and compare notes on, and she produced her mobile phone and scrolled through her photos too.

Because I had positioned myself around to her side of the table, I could touch her as we looked at our phones. It helped to create a little more connection and avoid the date becoming too much of a Sunday-morning social, but eventually we ran out of photos and we lapsed back into awkwardness. I was then perched next to her, looking over her, and the physical dynamics suddenly felt wrong.

So I declared, "Let's go for a walk."

We walked out of the shopping center and around the park outside, and it freed up the situation. At least a little. I then found myself giving her an English lesson, and talking very slowly in order to do so. That seemed to help, and for a few minutes, we did actually enjoy a walk together. I even put my arm out, and she took it. But then we reached a point, having gone one lap around the small park, where it felt really awkward again. She had, you will recall, been teetering on the edge of her seat with her handbag in her lap ready to go at any moment, and I think she felt that she had already spent too long and got too intimate with me on a first date.

Then we reached the final awkward moment where we said goodbye to one another. We did a stupid air kiss – any sort of actual kissing was totally out of the question, of course, as she was not relaxed and the vibe was not at all there – and walked off in opposite directions. She to the station and me back to my flat.

There was quite a lot of texting afterwards, and looking back on it now, I am surprised I was not able to get her out on a second date. Working against me were two factors. The first was simple logistics. She lived in another city and this meant date requests were complicated. On one occasion I did actually line up a date in her city, as I happened to know another girl from the past who worked at a restaurant there, and I used this to explain why I would be in Bialystok. But I never really intended to meet this girl from the restaurant. Unfortunately, I could not quite make it work. This is close as it came. Having told her I was coming up for the weekend to visit my friend who worked in a restaurant, here is how the rest of the conversation went:

Her: But I'm working this weekend in my office...and meeting with my family...so I don't know...sunday at 8am and saturday at 22pm so maybe next week...Monday is better for me.
Me: Monday I'm back in Warsaw. No time on Sunday?
Her: No :(

And so it petered out.

Or did it?

Well, in fact, in between writing drafts of this chapter and a good nine months after the date itself, I actually bumped into her in the same shopping centre where we had originally met. The conversation was quite lively, albeit short, and I was quick-witted enough to put in a long time constraint when I told her, "I'm pretty busy this month, but perhaps next month we can grab a drink and catch up." When we wondered out loud whether we still had each other's phone numbers and she put her hand in her pocket to get out her phone, I gestured for her to put it away.

"I'm sure I've got your number," I said.

As of this writing, the texting has been strong and she has even just suggested a date to meet when she is next in Warsaw, so it is quite likely that we may yet go on a second date, probably almost a year after the first.

Is an awkward date a bad date?

Before I get onto the main reflection of this date, let's discuss a couple of simple points that will help make dates easier. These are "Must Dos!"

The first is to have a bunch of fun photos on your phone that you can show any girl any time. The second is to have Google translate on your phone. Both require relatively minimum investment of time and energy and could really help you out during difficult periods on the date. You're not Casanova yet, and don't be an arrogant prick and think you don't need these aids! I spent 15 years being an arrogant prick and thought that I did not need to learn this stuff. In fact, I thought that there was nothing much to learn anyway. It's painful for me to think of how much time I lost.

And if you think that Google translate does not work, then please wait to read the later dates in this series, particularly the ones in Russia, to see just how powerful a date can be without either of you speaking a word of each other's language.

The second, and main, reflection I have is that just because a date is awkward does not necessarily mean that the girl is not interested. It could, in fact, be quite the reverse. I gave up on Date 6, partly because of the problem of her living in another city, but partly because of the awkwardness, which I interpreted as being a bad sign. We had "nothing in common," I told myself, or "It's too much like hard work," or even, "She's clearly not interested and just enjoying a cup of coffee with a guy for fun."[4]

You may recall that I had had a brilliant date with Date 3, Portugal Girl, and yet ultimately it all went nowhere. The big lesson is that you should not judge a date by how it "feels." Just because it has been terribly awkward, you should not decide that the girl is not interested or that you are not making progress or that it's "going badly." This is an erroneous link in the chain of thinking, and a link that I suspect, if the rest of the male world is anything at all like me, is not infrequently made.

Indeed, there is an argument to say that awkwardness is good. You as a guy need to learn to ride it out and be happy to bear it for as long as is needed and simply not to react to it. Reacting to it in this instance would have been making inane conversation just for the sake of filling the void or silence.

---

[4] If a girl has showed up for a date, especially if she has dressed up like Date 6 had, it is "on." And yet a guy will sit there and do mental yoga, contorting himself into a position where he actually starts to believe that it is just clearly a social, friendly meeting and there is no sexual chemistry whatsoever.

In the case of these two dates, it was clear that they were young and gauche and that this was always going to be a problem.

Young girls who just may be shy about the whole experience and naive sexually just need a lot of comfort first. I remember a buddy telling me about his experience with one girl where she was saying nothing and being very shy, and he was basically just walking her around a park, perhaps touching hands once or twice and then almost going back to the drawing board for the next date. And the next. And the next...

But *eventually* she relaxed and *eventually* he got her back to his apartment and *eventually* they made sweet love.

The trick here was to put her at her ease and just take it real slow. Also, keeping the dates short, if necessary, can give her the illusion of having known you for longer.

Don't rule out an awkward date. Be patient. Even an Ice Age has to thaw. *Eventually.*

Date 7: "The Girl with No Name"

I met "The Girl With No Name" in a city square, and what drew me to her was her great physique. She stood elegantly and confidently next to a tram stop, talking on a mobile phone, while her long, red hair blew lightly in the breeze.

The approach was fun and playful. After she "hooked" and started to ask me questions about myself, I took her hand and introduced myself. This is a good excuse to create a physical connection. She held my hand for some time.

And then after a little banter and a good amount of flirtation I asked for her number and got out my phone.

As we were putting each other's numbers into our phones, I saw her hesitate and teased her:

"Do remember my name?"

"Oh." A pause. She laughed and then looked apologetic. "No."

"I don't believe it!" I declared. "I only told you a few moments ago!"

"Alex," I said, helping her type in the digits.

But it wasn't her poor memory which was to play such a key part in the date that followed...

* * *

The first date took place not far from where we had met. In fact, I think that if you are struggling to think of a date location, it is not a bad idea to simply tell the girl to meet you where you initially met. We went to a bar at a funky, warehouse-y complex, and once there, jumped onto bar stools and began chatting. It was only going well – the location was good and the bar stools made it easy to touch her from time to time and make a physical connection. She was wearing a sort of azure-blue necklace that made her look like Cleopatra, so I could easily reach forward and touch her necklace and tease her about looking like an ancient Egyptian (and a notoriously hot one, at that).

It all seemed to be going well… so I pushed it one step further. I "spiked" up the conversation.[5]

The way I did it on this occasions was to get her to stand up, suddenly complimenting her on her elegant stature.

"You know, what I noticed about you…when we first met…" I said, gradually.

"Yes?" she said, curious.

"In the street – I was actually some distance away from you in the square…"

"What did you notice?"

"Your stature – well, posture. The way you carried yourself caught my eye. I bet you were an athlete or a high-jumper or something when you were young. I like it."

---

[5] Spikes are some of the first thing you learn when you learn about daygame, because, unlike in a bar or club, it may not be so easily to create a physical sexual connection. During the daytime or on a first date, you do it verbally or physically, just a few times during the date, pushing it and coming out of your comfort zone for a moment, before rolling off and returning to normal conversation. I learned about spikes from Tom Torero's early material. I just have a few basic ones, like in this story, that I repeatedly use.

"Oh, well," she began, bubbling away. "I was an ice skater when I was young. And we trained, regularly, with a real tough lady teacher. She was Czech."

"So… you took it quite seriously?"

"Oh, yes."

"As a career?"

"Yes."

And then she drooped a little.

"But… I don't know… it didn't work out."

"But you're quite tall for an ice skater, surely? I mean, you know, like these Chinese girls and whatnot, they have to be super tiny so the dudes in the stretchy, shiny leotards can fling them around like tinsel. I'm not saying you weren't talented or determined, but you're being a little hard on yourself, because you've got to be pretty lucky, physically, and if you're not, you can end up throwing your life into it and become terribly disillusioned. It's a short shelf-life for an athlete. You're probably best out of it."

She seemed reassured and I left my hand on her leg as I made the speech for emphasis (and also because, of course, she had nice legs and I wanted to touch them). [6]

There was a pause. We were both relaxed. It was about thirty or forty minutes into the date and the ice was broken. We took sips of our drinks…

Now, before I go any further, I should just explain that while I was getting ready for the date, which on this occasion I did with military precision (there is nothing worse than messing up a date just because you missed out on basic preparation), I

---

[6] Incidentally, there is a photo of this girl on the vlog I recorded on my YouTube channel.

realized with alarm that I had forgotten her name. *Hang on! It will be in my phone,* I said to myself. I checked, but it wasn't. These days if it is just a street number that I got, I don't usually bother putting the name in right away, but I will usually type her name into a draft message, like, "Hey Claudia, unexpected but fun meeting you earlier." After all, you never know whether they are going to flake on the date. But in this instance I hadn't drafted a text at all.

I then said to myself, *So what? What does it matter? I mean, just run with it. People forget each other's names all the time. In fact,* I said to myself, *why not just make a virtue out of it and experiment. Just throw the fact of it into the conversation and be bold as brass and see what comes. Make light of it. After all, what is the big deal? It's not like she's your sister or something!*

It's a rather basic error that most guys make, of course, because they think that women think like men. Or should, at least. Men projecting men-thinking onto women is one of the classic errors men make. It's probably the underlying cause of frustration when a man, sometimes even with pride, declares, "I don't understand women!" In other words, if you had met a man and forgotten his name, or even if you had forgotten your best friend's name, it would be a subject of great hilarity but of no consequence.

So, I shrugged it off with a smile, slightly smug and pleased with myself that I was showing such bravado.

So, back to the date. I put down my drink. I leaned back, confident and cocky.

"You know what?" I said. "I don't remember your name?"

A beat.

She stared.

I shrugged. I took another sip, a little more nervously this time, a tremor of anxiety suddenly running through me. This particular silence seemed like a different brand of the usual silence, and rather than it pumping up the tension and being sexy, it felt scary. My remark hung in the air, like one of those petite Chinese ice skaters who had been thrown up high by her partner, and there she spins, like a helicopter, pirouetting high up into the sky. Watching this, you take a sharp intake of breath, wondering whether or not she is going to come crashing down.

Well, to stretch the analogy further, I don't think the judges on this occasion would have lifted up a row of five perfect 10s for me. The fall was painful.

"You don't remember my name?"
"Nope. Not at all. Isn't it funny? Completely left my mind!"

She stared some more and blinked.

Thinking back on it, she might well have thought that the way I expressed myself was a bit cocky and arrogant, whereas in my own mind I was just "being honest."[7]

"I don't believe it," she said. "Do you often approach girls in the street?"

She was suddenly suspicious and I replied by qualifying and agreeing, "Oh, yes, you were number 38, hahaha!"

But the old favorite didn't work this time. Instead, it sounded

---

[7] Oh, how poorly misunderstood is that expression, along with that other old favorite, "just be yourself"!

hollow and out of place in the context of the conversation.

She now clearly had the idea that I had approached lots of girls, but it was not in a good way. I had not anticipated this as the consequence of my honesty. She now may have thought that I was just a random weirdo who approached people in the street. I said, "Finish up!" and announced that we were going. I paid, and there was another long period of silence as I completed that transaction and then we left.

We walked side by side. Now the next venue was a little way, as the square where we were was not close to my flat on this occasion, so we had quite a walk. And as hard as I tried to talk about other topics, every time it all came round to that. And it just hung in the air, like a sword over me, the whole walk. The walk was a good fifteen minutes, which felt like an age.

On the way, she teased me, because, as she pointed out, "I can't believe you forgot, because of what happened."

"What do you mean?" I ventured, feeling like, although I was already in a corner, I was going to get squeezed in even tighter.

"You don't remember?"

What can she possibly mean? I wondered. *I mean, I've stopped about 45 other girls since I stopped her, I can't remember every conversation!*

"In the street," she continued. "Our conversation?"

I tried to recollect what she was talking about. The trouble was I had been on a lot of dates. In the future, I would actually record short voice memos on my phone after getting a number in order to reflect on what had happened. But for now, I could remember nothing, and all my approaches were jumbled up together.

She decided she was going to milk it. When I put my arm around her for a moment she pulled away.

"I guess you have just spoken to a lot of girls and you're just mixed up, right? But what is surprising to me is the way you gave *me* such a hard time."

We walked a few moments more.

"It's not far," I said, ignoring her taunts. "Just up here."

"You told me off for not remembering your name, don't you remember?"

It slowly dawned on me. I had completely forgotten about the conversation in the street. My mind did a triple axel as I thought, *Oh shit, this is bad. She has totally got the frame and is nailing me.*

"Yes," she said, driving home her point."I can't believe you've forgotten."

We walked some more, this time in silence, and I wondered what I was going to do. It did not feel as if I could leave it and totally ignore it. Anyway, I had tried changing the subject, and it just snapped back to this topic every time. I decided that the best thing to do was simply to make an apology and be sincere. And so as we got to the corner where we had to turn. We both stopped and I said, "Look, I'm sorry about the whole name thing. I forgot. But, you know, I like you. I've enjoyed your company, and I'd like to hang out with you some more. So if you want to grab a quick drink, I know a nice little bar down here."

And I held out my hands and shrugged.

She now went "coquettish." It was like her feathers suddenly preened themselves out in a colorful fan. She lifted her head and said, "I don't know. I think I might go home… it's a week night and I have work early."

She hesitated, but I was not about to try to bring her round again (nor was a I capable of doing so at that moment), and so I simply said, slightly annoyed at her coquettish reaction to my plain-speaking, "Okay, let's go. I'll walk you to the metro."

We arrived at the metro entrance, and at the top of the steps, she paused before leaving. By this point, I felt she had gone too far, and I was just pissed off that she was milking it so much. I suddenly started feeling annoyed with her behavior. *I don't need this. She's not all that hot - nice figure but not totally hot - and I've got options right now. I actually think she's being a bit of a bitch.*

And so I said something short like, "Okay, well, have a good week." And I felt that I had sounded pretty final.

But somehow she seemed to misunderstand me, and she said, "Maybe, we'll see."

She had obviously thought I had said something like, "See you next week." English was not her first language. She was Polish.

She was being coquettish again.

I just walked off, and she walked down into the metro.

I decided afterwards that I should not just be following up with every girl, and I talked with a mate and he found her reaction a bit over the top, totally milking the whole silly thing, and so I decided that that was it - I would not see her again. This project was not purely about escalating with every girl, but about keeping an eye on and being discriminating about the girls as longer-term partnership material. *Some girls just think they're so special and love to jump on a guy if he so much as puts a single foot wrong. Who do they think they are? They'll be more forgiving when they're 40, by which time it will be too late to have*

learned the lesson that they can't just get away with bad behavior!
And I never did text her.

Owning your mistakes

There are two different sorts of musings I have after writing up this date. The first is to step back and look at it on a purely practical level and to see what can be learned for next time. There are perhaps three different things that I could have done. What do you vote for?

1. Not bring up the fact you have forgotten her name at all and hope it doesn't come up;

2. Find a cunning way to find out her name. For example, asking for her help with the spelling so you can write it in your phone; or

3. Be open and honest about it and simply ask her what her name is as you've forgotten.

Well, the answer is, of course, none of the above.

Before I discuss what I think is the right answer, it is just first worth stating the obvious, which is that you should try to avoid ending up in that position in the first place! Obviously, as men, we are renowned for not listening to women and this is the first lesson to learn. I simply should have listened. And one practical answer for the future, which I have adopted, is to make a voice memo of every conversation I have with a girl who gives me her number. This helps me to really reflect on what has happened. It is all very well to get excited about the fact you have gotten a girl's number, but there is a lot further to go on the date. I guess some guys might prefer keeping a journal or something like that. But just "becoming a good listener" will never work without some method.[8]

The second, more important, musing I had about this date was that at the end of the day, you are going to make mistakes.[9] A girl is going to test your frame and the way you respond to your own cock-ups is as important as not making them in the first place, if not more important.

It is important to recognize that what is very unattractive to a woman is a guy who backtracks or apologizes for himself, and we need to accept that we will all make mistakes, but the important thing is that we must **own** them. Now, in my case, I perhaps affected a carelessness and bravado, but it was quite reactive. I was preempting the danger of being found out by boldly announcing it, which is perhaps better than nervously squirming about forgetting her name and apologizing profusely, but reactive nonetheless.

Rather than do nothing and wait for it to go away (as in the

---

[8] Does this seem all rather contrived? Well, the whole thing is contrived! I mean, whether it is following a structure or routine on the date or during the approach. If you are reading this book, you have accepted that these are skills that you need to learn and structures or principles that you need to follow. You can choose to stay with the idea that dating is all some sort of "beautiful synchronicity" in which two people meet and there is chemistry and sparks fly and absolutely no work is required. Or, if you are reading this book, you are probably now healthily skeptical about this and realize that work needs to be done.

[9] I have been reading Kezia Noble's book, *The Noble Art of Seducing Women*. In one anecdote she points out that if you make a mistake, that is fine, but it is how you handle the mistake that is the key thing.

first option above), I should not just wait for it to come up, because I know, as a confident guy, that I can deal with it – and make a virtue of it to boot.

So what would this have actually looked like? Well, it would have been better to spin it around in a self-amused way. It occurs to me that self-amusement is a good touchstone here. For example, let's assume she had raised it or it had come up in conversation, I could have spun it like this:

"You know what, I've actually forgotten. I think it's like – during my time in the Korean War, I got a bit of shrapnel lodged in my brain, and I've had blackouts ever since and can't remember the names of the girls I've been with. Not one. Terrible."

"Oh right…" she is already smirking. "You don't remember the names of any of the girls you've slept with?"

"Irresponsible, I know. I'm a pig. In fact, frankly I don't know why you are having anything to do with me. Take your chance before it's too late. I would leave now if I were you. And by the way, I'm also a classic, lazy, beer-drinking British male with the memory of a goldfish. Look, I don't want you telling me later you haven't been warned."

And you smirk. And she smiles…

I was also reactive in another way, of course, like we so often are as human beings. I got annoyed, and in order to protect my ego, I decided to shut her out. She had been a bit too coquettish, and it was not impressive, but so what? What am I here to do if it's not to learn to become better at dating and seduction? It was too early to reach that decision anyway, and I was making a snap judgment off of one short date and one incident. I might

22

as well have decided she was not the girl of my dreams *after* I had fooled around with her. So, I reacted.

Looking back on it, it was once more a painful lesson in the importance of rolling off, shrugging your shoulders, and taking the hit. And then perhaps making a positive out of it by responding in a self-amused way with a smile. It might well have made her more attracted, rather than less.

Date 8: Monty The Python, or "When was the last time you had sex?"

I met Date 8 in a Cafe Nero in the center of town, and we had had a good conversation. It was one of those situations that had arisen very naturally – I was working in the morning on my laptop. She was not acting so naturally, however, but busy moving furniture around in a rather energetic fashion. We were the only two in the mezzanine area of the cafe. She was a confident and spirited girl and had a nice figure.

I opened up a conversation, and it turned out she was actually getting ready for a job interview and was paranoid about the position of her and her prospective boss. We chatted for a while and then exchanged numbers, and I wished her luck in the interview.[10]

I did not get her out on a date straight away. It had been a solid interaction and there was no rush. In fact, I forgot about her. And then a few weeks later, a girl waved at me in the mezzanine area of Cafe Nero one morning, and I realized that it was the same girl.

---

[10] Come to think of it, even from that initial moment, I should have realized that there was something unique and special about this girl! Moving sofas around at 8am in the morning was a bit "hyper."

In the run up to the date, she actually phoned me a couple of times. I do not think this had ever happened to me before or since. She was definitely one for "frame control," although it was not a conscious thing. She just she had a lot of energy about her and perhaps she was also nervous.

The second time she phoned was actually on the afternoon of the date, and she wanted to change the time and the venue. She did not want to meet in a bar in the evening around 6pm, but instead suggested meeting in The Palace of Culture in the cinema coffee shop. And she wanted to change the time to 5pm and wanted to emphasize that it was "just for coffee." So I acquiesced rather than get into a debate about it.

* * *

When I showed up for the date, she was already there, sitting in a sofa in the far corner. I noticed this high level of energy once more, the energy that had been there during that morning when she had been rearranging furniture. She sort of "jumped up" and wanted to order the drinks immediately. She ordered a hot chocolate, and by the time we had paid, someone else had unfortunately stolen our sofa. So we ended up in full view of everyone at the entrance on a table with two chairs, beneath a row of photos of the famous actor, Steve McQueen, looking down on us. It was tricky. She was clearly either completely new to this or just a crazy high-octane character.

We talked about something or other, but I cannot remember what, just social chit chat, before I decided to try playing "the truth game." But when I started to explain the rules, she wanted to change them all.

"So you have three questions and I have three questions…"

"Why? Why three?"

"Well, you can have more if you like… so you can ask anything if you like or you can refuse to answer. But if you refuse to answer you have to drink a shot of vodka."

"Why vodka? I don't like vodka. Why can't it be some chocolate cake?"

"You can't have chocolate cake! That defeats the whole point of the game. It's got to be a forfeit. Not something you really, really like."

We started to try and play, but it was no use. I should have learned my lesson by now that it is best to either informally slide into the truth game or, when the mood is not right, not to do it too early. The wheels came off this topic and we sat there, not in silence, but just saying stuff to each other like tennis players hitting balls over the net, with no real communication. The conversation was superficial.

Eventually we got round to the topic of sports, and it seemed as if this was something she was genuinely interested in. I guessed she had been a bit of a tomboy when she was younger. She was certainly very energetic. She had, by this point, told me she had two jobs, not one, and she now told me that she was also a semi-professional snooker player! Her week must have been like a whirlwind.

I mentioned to her that when I was a boy, I used to love watching snooker on the telly and used to spend hours doing so, usually at night after my mother had turned the lights off. Snooker had just "arrived" with the advent of a show called, "Pot Black," which was on BBC2 at the time and was a very popular show. She had actually heard of it, which, considering she was far too young to have ever seen it, as well as the fact she was also Polish, was remarkable.

She also remembered the famous snooker final between Steve Davis and Dennis Taylor in 1985, which was almost certainly before she was born. And it was there that somehow the conversation and the date came alight. It was because I found – in a topic area of interest to her – something that also really interested and amused me.

"It's incredible, but you know that the show was watched by about 18 million, which would be unheard of now on live television. It went on for two days. A marathon. And it went to the final black! Of 35 frames. Do you remember that dude, Dennis something, with the huge glasses that he used to peer over as he was drawing back the snooker cue, and they were sort of cut off at the top so he could see over them when he was potting, presumably."

"Oh, yes! Dennis Taylor!"

"You saw it?!"

"I've seen it, yes – obviously not at the time."

"But you know, thinking about it, the really amazing thing was the show itself. I mean, can you imagine the conversation between the producer who came up with the idea and the television executives he must have persuaded? Imagine trying to persuade them today:

"So I've got this great idea for a television show. Sports."

"Okay, great. What's the idea?" ask the eager commissioning executives.

"So we get these guys, dressed in weird dinner suits, black waistcoats and they play snooker."

"Snooker?"

"Yeah. Snooker. With balls. You know, like pool but it goes on a lot longer."

"How long?"

"Well, a match is about 35 frames..."

"Frames?"

"Games."

"How long is that going to take?"

"Could be like five hours or something."

"Jesus. Five hours!"

And a second executive around the table pipes up. "So, what is the viewer looking at exactly, I mean, what's the production setup?"

"Well, obviously we'll have a camera setup of the players, and then the main one is just over the table itself, so you can see the whole table."

"So like we watch from above, looking down a green table and watch balls being potted into holes? And it lasts five hours..."

"On average. Sometimes they last a couple of days."

"And what time were you thinking this would air? I mean, it's sort of graveyard slot territory early morning, right, for insomniacs?"

"Well, no. After the watershed, sure, but I was still thinking around prime time, 9 or 10pm."

"I don't know how that producer sold it. He needs a medal," I finished.

She was now laughing and suddenly, as so often happens in dates, the ice had broken and we were talking freely. And I don't know what it was exactly, but now she started talking about herself quite a lot. Certain interesting facts about her started to come out, as I sat there sipping my glass of whisky and she sat there with her hot chocolate.

28

She moved on from snooker, and I asked her, now drifting back onto the truth game, "Are you a dog person or a cat person?"

"Mmm..." she thought. "I prefer dogs but not those little things you stuff in a lady's handbag. I can't see the point."

"I agree," I said. "A dog should be a proper dog. Like for hunting, rounding up sheet or something, or killing burglars. So do you have a dog?"

"No," she said. "I have a rat."

"Ah," I said with faint surprise. "Really?"

I don't know why I should have expressed any surprise at all. I mean, rats are probably like pigs, I said to myself, perfectly respectable and very clean and hygienic creatures. They just have a bad rap from humans.

"Yes," she continued, "... and a python."

"Ah!" I said, trying to conceal yet more surprise. I floundered for a response. "Does that work? I mean, is that a good idea?"

"Obviously not in the same tank," she said, slightly tartly. "But actually they do get on. It was quite funny..." she continued, coming up with a story of her own. "But I went to the pet shop recently – you know, to buy some mice."

"Of course," I said.

"So I wanted to get about a dozen..."

"Yep."

"But then the pet shop owner was a bit suspicious. Why did I want that many? he asked. But what business was it of his! I thought. Well, he didn't actually ask, but I could see it on his face, you know? That he really wanted to ask me what I was going to do with twelve mice. He was obviously thinking. He

29

was really reluctant to give me any."

Suddenly she became animated and hyper.

"But what business is it of his?! He's in the business of selling animals and stuff and making money. He should be grateful that I'm buying a large quantity. I should get a discount."

"Live mice?" I asked.

"Of course."

"No, sure." I nodded.

"Monty won't eat dead ones."

"So they were for the python?"

"Yes," she said, "for Monty."

"Monty is the name of the python?"

"Yes. I just told you!" she blurted out.

Interesting girl, I thought to myself. I sat there, struggling with my prejudices. *Some people liked snakes and rats. What's wrong with that? And a python needed to eat like anything else.*

But I also felt that this was a slightly exceptional girl and not one who was especially into boyfriends and dating, and it was starting to feel like one of the most non-sexual dates I had ever had. And it was going south. I mean, there had been very little flirting, if any, and it all seemed way too social. I decided really had to spike it up somehow. (After having first getting off the conversation of rats and pythons.) But it was not a good situation, as we had lost the nice big sofa and were stuck sitting across from each other in a busy area near the entrance.

I carefully reviewed my options... *Should I lean across the table and take her hands, or suggest that she has nice hands, or perhaps palm read her hands? Or say that she looks like a musician. No, no, no, no. That doesn't work. She's sporty. And anyway, it's far too wide a table. It would be really awkward leaning over.*

So it would have to be verbal escalation. And I considered that we had been playing touch and go with the truth game, so perhaps now was the moment to ask another question. She was bubbling away, and I interrupted her, "Listen, we've forgotten the truth game, we each have one more question…"

"Okay," she said. "I can't think of anything. You ask?"

Except this time I needed to take a risk and really push the boat out. I needed to sexualize the truth game more. Much more.

I looked at her long and hard, formulating my truth-game question. Finally, I looked her in the eye and asked her,

"When was the last time you had sex?"

She stared at me for a few micro-moments.

"Sorry?"

"Sex. When was the last time."

She got up, grabbed her coat, saying,

"Er… that's…sorry, that's too much. I'm out."

And she walked out.

I stared into my glass, perplexed. I stared up at the photos of Steve McQueen above the table, looking down at me. One of them was him in a sports car, a classic in black and white, looking at the camera with an alarmed expression.

Is it okay to talk about sex?

Now, when a guy starts out on this stuff, he probably needs to sexualize his interactions with girls a lot more than he has been doing up until that point. He has probably been very social and has put himself into a friend-zone time and again. He probably should say stuff like, "When was the last time you had sex?" just to experiment and get himself out of his old comfort zone.

But, of course, this needs a massive qualification. And the point here is to acknowledge that there is a world of difference between generating a sexual vibe and making it clear that you are interested in a girl sexually and actually talking about sex. I think it is a whole lot better talking about sex than your job, your relationship history, or about politics and religion, and this is why, perhaps initially, you should dive in and be provocative. It is certainly one way to spike up a conversation. Also, a guy who can talk about sex freely and without inhibition is probably attractive to women in so far as he communicates he is relaxed about it and probably has experience with it.

It is, of course, such a fine line, and you risk crossing that line into being crude and making the girl feel uncomfortable. You also risk showing the girl too early that you want to have sex with her and are attracted to her which takes out any flirting and mystery. But of course if you are confident talking about sex then go for it.

But if it comes to that second venue, and you are in a quiet corner in a sofa, or if you have go her back to your flat, then hopefully you will be generating a sexual vibe without talking about it. You keep the subject of sex covert, but make sure the girl knows that it is there, simmering under the surface. As with flirting, in which you raise the promise of sex with the guarantee of it, it seems that the best way to proceed with girls is covert, hinting at it or raising the possibility of it without actually ever saying it. Certainly until you get to know her better or have already slept with her. PUAs are all clear that a guy needs to show his sexual intent, but this does not necessarily, or perhaps rarely, mean that he needs to talk about having sex.

Further, if you do raise it – or ask a question that is sexually provocative during a game like the truth game, as I did here – it is better done so once the ice is well and truly broken.

My conclusion with this question and particularly in the context of Date 9 is that the key issue is calibration. Calibration is both knowing when to escalate and when to roll off as well as reading the situation and knowing how far you can take it. Only an idiot would ever say, "Never talk about sex," or "Never reveal to a girl in conversation that you are sexually interested in her." The point is that at times it actually might or even will be appropriate. It truly is a case of calibration, and this can only be discovered through experience.

As guys we have to escalate, but we often do not know when and how much, and the truth is we are probably going to break a lot of eggs along the way. So in the case of Date 9, I make no apologies for being bold and getting rejected. It is better to take a chance by trying something and risk being burned than it is to play it safe. Although Date 9 was one of my more spectacular achievements in this regard. (Though by no means my most spectacular.[11])

END OF PART 3

---

[11] See Chapter 12 of my first book, "Too Late, Mate?"

Note on Authenticity

I thought I should write an end note on the authenticity of the stories in the book. I have actually taken great pains to ensure that all the stories are accurate, and I recorded vlogs after each first date and also occasional updates (see my YouTube Channel, "52 First Dates"). I also did voice memos after all the approaches in order to document this journey. This was primarily for my own benefit, in order to reflect and learn, but it also has ensured the accuracy of the books. The text messages are all verbatim, hence the occasional spelling mistake. Rest assured that these stories are "as it happened".

12246558R00025

Printed in Germany
by Amazon Distribution
GmbH, Leipzig